100 THINGS TO DO WHEN YOU'RE DEAD

100 THINGS TO DO WHEN YOU'RE DEAD

Rob Bailey

MICHAEL O'MARA BOOKS LIMITED

First published in Great Britain in 2008 by
Michael O'Mara Books Limited
9 Lion Yard
Tremadoc Road
London SW4 7NQ

A CIP catalogue record for this book is available from the British Library

ISBN 978-1-84317-337-3

10 9 8 7 6 5 4 3 2 1
Designed by Ana Bjezancevic/Design 23

Printed and bound in Italy by L.E.G.O.

INTRODUCTION

In 1789, Benjamin Franklin wrote the line, 'In this world nothing can be said to be certain, except death and taxes'. This is undoubtedly a clever phrase, but it is somewhat fatalistic and seems to miss the upside of death – namely, no taxes! Excepting any bothersome details of inheritance tax, most tax obligations expire when you do. In this sense, death is very liberating to you and to those around you.

There are many functions that a dead person can capably fulfil, perhaps earning a good wage for friends and relatives at the same time. Why not fill in for a traffic cop sitting at the side of a motorway? Or help enrich your friend's compost? You could make yourself helpful around the house. Maybe you could become a celebrity – everyone deserves their fifteen minutes of fame – don't miss out just because you've died.

With a little effort, a dead person will even get to take part in careers and activities they missed out on in life. Death takes the risk out of things that you might have been too afraid to do when alive: if you've been drawn to abseiling but were afraid of heights, now it's only a tall building and a rope away (and there'll be no need to bother with health and safety forms); if you always wanted to compete in a Swiss stone-tossing competition, take the strain out of it and be a substitute for the stone.

Here are 100 useful, productive, and often money-spinning ideas for how your body could be put to use when you've spent your last breath. If you've left debts or unfulfilled ambitions behind you, and you've no obligation to be buried before sunset, then find the solutions to your woes in the following pages. Life is short and modern times encourage us to cram in as much as possible; but death lasts for infinity, so allow yourself to relax during life – achieve what you can – then embrace infinity, knowing that there's still more to be accomplished.

This book is ideal for:

BEREAVED LOVED ONES

GRIEVING FAMILIES

PEOPLE CONSIDERING DYING

Parents will be able to rest easy, knowing that you won't get shirty or demand a taxi home just because they linger a little longer over their romantic dinner.

HELP FRIENDS WITH BABYSITTING

BE AN ARTIST'S MODEL

You won't cramp the potential of a future Michelangelo by fidgeting.

JOIN THE BLAIR WITCH PROJECT APPRECIATION SOCIETY

Surprise your loved ones by paying a light-hearted tribute to your favourite horror film.

BECOME A BATHROOM TIDY

Lighthouse-shaped tidies, mirrored cabinets and glass shelves are *so* last year. No one is going to look more up-to-date than the proud homeowner with a corpse bathroom tidy.

BE THE BEST MAN AT A WEDDING

The groom will be able to relax, knowing that you're not going to say anything embarrassing.

BECOME A CONTESTANT ON *BIG BROTHER*

Dead bodies have been known to have muscle spasms, which push air from the lungs, forcing out groans and scary, incomprehensible utterances. You'd fit right in on *Big Brother*.

JOIN A BATTLE RE-ENACTMENT SOCIETY

You won't mind playing dead in a muddy field from the first minute of the first battle.

BE A BURGLAR DETERRENT

A corpse deterrent will ring alarm bells without disturbing
the neighbours.

BECOME A BUTLER

What could impress your friends' dates more than their very own butler?

BECOME A BOUNCER

You'll be patient and gentlemanly – and if anyone pushes you too far all you'll do is fall over.

BE A BOTTLE OPENER

Quality organic ale? Quality organic bottle opener.

BECOME A BIKE RACK

When every other parking space
is taken you'll be the perfect bike
rack – portable, with integral wheel
locator, and you're more than likely
to put off any potential thief.

BUY CIGARETTES AND ALCOHOL FOR KIDS

Encourage responsible drinking and smoking by helping
children demystify these things at an early age. Simply pop into
the offy with the right cash and a shopping list round your neck.

TAKE PART IN A CABER TOSS

See the Highland Games from a new perspective.

GO BODY SURFING

You'll not be waving or drowning – just surfing.

'Yes – that's right – he's the embodiment of dedication. Worked right round the clock on your motor. He does us proud.'

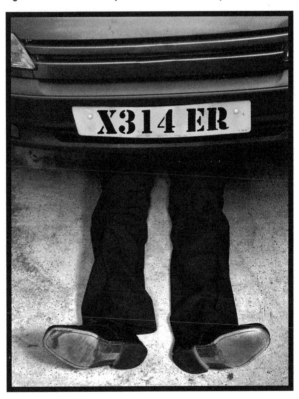

HELP FRIENDS WITH CAR SHARING

Help lady friends feel at ease when driving alone, and enable them to whiz freely down the car-share lane.

MODEL FOR A MAIL-ORDER CATALOGUE

Key skills – pointing and adopting a distant stare.
You'll excel yourself.

BE A BUOY

Is that a buoy?
No, it's a man.

BECOME A COFFEE TABLE

This classy furniture is guaranteed to be a conversation piece.

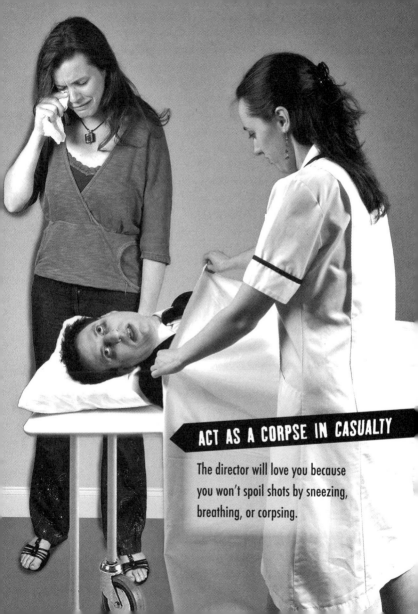

ACT AS A CORPSE IN CASUALTY

The director will love you because
you won't spoil shots by sneezing,
breathing, or corpsing.

You'll be a calming influence on over-excitable children.

Your deathly stare will put daytime viewers at ease – it's called mirroring.

Dead people don't need botox to help them keep the same rigid face for hours of inane television.

Star Buy!

Matching embroidere

Call Now

handbag and bracelet

BE A CRAZY GOLF OBSTACLE

Because it's just not really crazy enough.

PLAY FOR THE ENGLAND CRICKET TEAM

Bring back the Ashes with some stiff competition.

PLAY IN A DEATH METAL BAND

Play to an audience highly appreciative of every death growl or morbid movement you make.

BECOME A DENTIST'S PRACTICE DUMMY

Let him get it all out of his system before working with
real patients.

SAVE THE BEST ROW IN THE CINEMA

Keep the best seats while your
friends stock up on popcorn
and pick'n'mix.

Ideal for dodging customs – you'll even come in your own tricky-to-search hard-case.

BECOME A DRUGS MULE

BECOME A DRAUGHT EXCLUDER

Endearing, functional and fun, you'll make the ideal housewarming present.

Death has boosted the career of many a star – perhaps it will give you your lucky break.

BECOME A YOUTUBE CELEB

01.26/08.45

Text Comments (214)

E-z-p1 (2 days ago)
I love the bit when the trolley rolls across the parking lot and out of the exit and it bumps into a curb and the body falls out of the trolley and the little old lady is so scared that she farts.

Prizoner Byte (a week ago)
dude,you haven't any idea

Badmoose (2 weeks ago)
AAAAAAAAAAAwsome!!!!!!!!!!!!!!!!

BE AN EXAMPLE TO OTHERS

This is what will happen to you if you ... smoke too much ...
drink too much ... have too much fun ...

BECOME A DAMIEN HIRST ARTWORK

There's not much more that cheeky Damien can do to shock us all, short of disembowelling himself and spilling his poo. Give him a hand, a leg up, and a shoo-in, and at the same time get preserved in a genuine work of art...

BECOME A FAST FOOD SERVER

Would you like flies with that?

WORK FOR AN ESCORT AGENCY

You can guarantee a happy
customer – she can yabber on all
night about anything she likes.

Be biofuel – without pushing world food prices up.

BE A SPONTANEOUS HUMAN COMBUSTION ENGINE

BE A FLOOD LEVEL MARKER

Locals will know they're
in trouble when you're
up to your eyeballs.

Empty coffins can be a little impersonal – make
them look more homely.

BE A SHIP'S FIGUREHEAD

You might have expired but you're not yet washed up.

BECOME A FOOTBALL MASCOT

Cuddly animals have been a bit
overdone – corpses haven't.

CLOSING DOWN GOLF SALE

REGENT STREET

1 MINUTE OXFORD STREET TUBE
FOLLOW MOBILE SIGNS

ADVERTISE A GOLF SALE

Which sport symbolizes the nearly dead more than golf?
Empathizing golfers will follow your signs like zombies.

BE A GARDEN GNOME

To some, the garden gnome is of poor taste – but who could say that about a corpse variation of the gnome (with a stylish bamboo fishing rod)?

GIVE GHOST TOURS

'Some of my best friends are ghosts.'

BECOME A GARGOYLE

You'll feel on top of the world.

BECOME A FOOTREST

Give your friends the support
they deserve.

WORK ON A GHOST TRAIN

A genuine scare will be a
welcome change from
being felt up in the dark by
a spotty teenage 'ghost'.

BECOME A HOODY

Hoodies are valued more than you might think – especially by politicians who like to take a pop at them. Be the ideal hoody: perfect to criticize without actually causing any trouble.

BE A SHOULDER TO CRY ON FOR THE WEEPIES

Legends of the Fall, Dirty Dancing, Brokeback Mountain, Titanic – you'll sit through them all back-to-back without thinking to complain once.

BECOME HOT AIR BALLOON BALLAST

There will be little debate here – it won't be Gandhi, Abraham Lincoln or Kylie going over the edge – it will be you.

BECOME A GOTH

You've got the dark clothes and the pale, deathly look – you'll be a natural.

My boyfriend didn't

Show how dignified you can be by not getting drawn into a full-on slanging match on national telly.

ll me he was dead

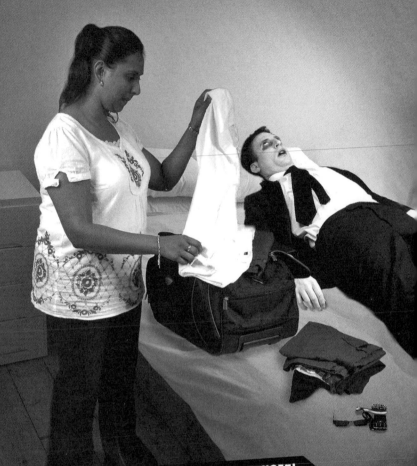

AVOID THE SINGLE SUPPLEMENT IN A HOTEL

'Yes – please send the bill to Mr Smith.'

Dying in the House of Lords is frowned upon, but merely
looking like you've departed this world is the norm.

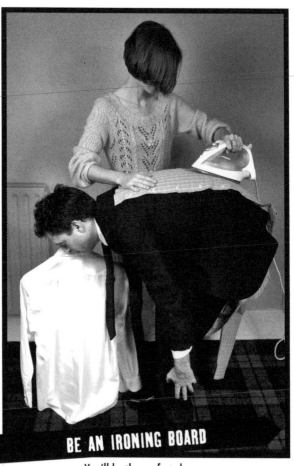

BE AN IRONING BOARD

You'll be the perfect shape.

EARN MONEY AS A HUMAN STATUE

Rigor mortis lasts about seventy-two hours – that's long enough to earn quite a few pennies.

BECOME AN ICE-SKATING PARTNER

Where in the rules does
it say that an ice-skating
partner can't be dead, or
hollowed out and stuffed,
for that matter?

WORK FOR AN IT HELPDESK

Adopt the three-finger salute of any self-respecting
helpdesk staff – Control, Alt, Delete.

BECOME A POKER CHAMP

Your poker face won't
give anything away.

DO JURY SERVICE

You'll have no need for Sudoku puzzles or an iPod
to get you through tedious fraud trials.

BECOME A JEWELLERY CADDY

Help make the most of jewellery –
enabling it to be proudly displayed
when not worn.

BECOME A LOLLIPOP LADY

Dead people don't need police checks before they can start work.

BECOME A MAKE-UP MODEL

It takes some experience to put on make-up effectively;
save sensitive skins the trauma of practice, and sensitive
souls the worry of looking like a clown.

MAKE THE NAUGHTY STEP MORE SCARY

Life's so scary these days that it's getting hard to frighten the children. With a genuine dead body on the naughty step, discipline will be a breeze.

BECOME A MAGICIAN'S ASSISTANT

The audience won't be able to work out how it's done – it's just a pity it will only be done once.

TAKE PART IN A POLICE LINE-UP

You won't spoil the line-up by
worrying about getting picked.

BECOME A SHOP MANNEQUIN

Anatomically correct and with real hair,
you'll outshine any other mannequin.

ACT ON MURDER MYSTERY WEEKENDS

In a weekend of hammy or wooden acting, you'll probably be the star of the show.

Play a supporting role in a TV soap - or for a barbecue.

No Animal
Experiments

Don't
experiment
on animlas
-
Experiment
on me

imal
ments

TAKE UP A POLITICAL CAUSE

Harshly, you will have forfeited
your right to vote by dying, but
you can still campaign or, in some
parts of the world, get elected.

KEEP OFF THE GRASS

NO BALL GAMES

CLEAR UP AFTER YOUR DOG

DON'T STARE AT THE FLOWERS

BECOME A PARK WARDEN

You'll be able to demonstrate the requisite level of humour for the role.

ATTEND A SÉANCE

Is anybody there? You'll be present in body, if not in spirit.

BE A SEESAW PARTNER

Parents can leave you both to play on the seesaw, knowing
that you'll be dependable and not send their precious
offspring back feeling sick.

PREACH ABOUT LIFE AFTER DEATH

How many preachers can claim first-hand experience of the afterlife?

BECOME A SANDBAG

Help combat the effects of global warming in an eco-friendly way. As freak weather causes more flooding, don't add a massive carbon footprint by carting sand around the world – be a local hero and become a sandbag.

WORK AS SANTA IN A GROTTO

If you've been good this year, Santa will be kind enough to not come around to visit.

HELP WITH TARGET PRACTISE

Will it be a case of Harold Godwinson in 1066 or
William Tell's son in 1307?

BECOME A SCARECROW

Farming's a hard life these days – if you gave a farmer your old clothes and a straw hat, they'd be more likely to put them on than use them for a scarecrow. You'll help a lot more by donating your body to ward vermin away from the farmer's precious crop.

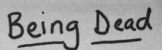

Being Dead

Pros
+
Peace

Cons
−
Lack
of mobility

RUN A SELF-HELP GROUP

Run a self-help group for coping with death.
Your quiet facilitation will be exemplary.

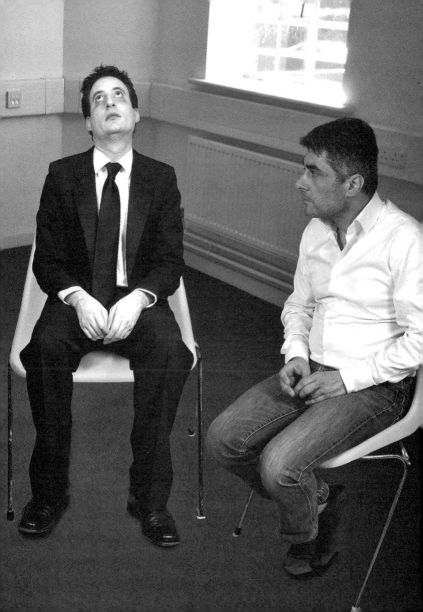

BECOME THE COMPETITIVE STARING WORLD CHAMP

You'll be a dead cert.

You won't disappoint
the kids by melting.

BE A STAND-IN BOYFRIEND

Your friend's mum will finally be able to stop worrying about her.

WORK AS A SPEED BUMP

The traffic will be much calmer.

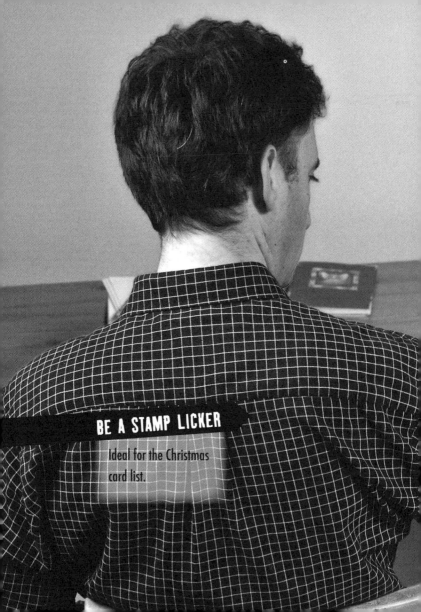

BE A STAMP LICKER

Ideal for the Christmas card list.

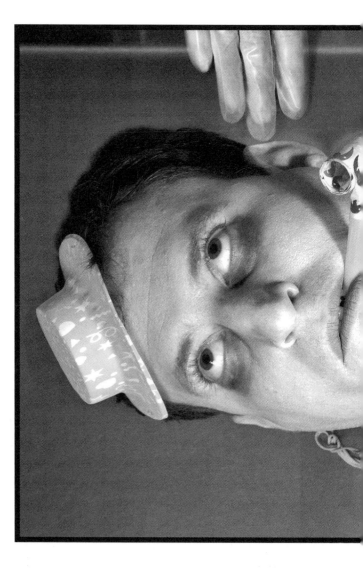

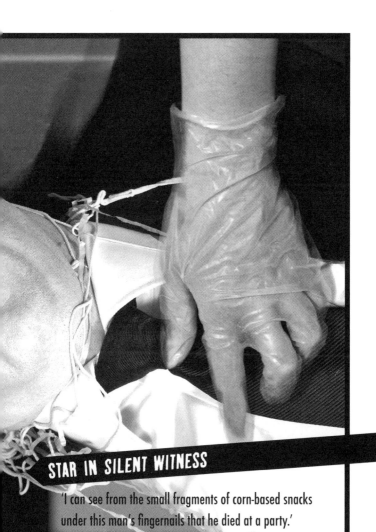

STAR IN SILENT WITNESS

'I can see from the small fragments of corn-based snacks under this man's fingernails that he died at a party.'

Double biology? This week rigor mortis and decomposition.

BECOME A SWIMMING POOL ATTENDANT

You can double as a float.

With you around, there's no need for a shy cyclist to go out on their own.

Who could be more accepting, tolerant and non-judgmental than a dead person? People love talking about themselves and you'll never offend them by interrupting.

BECOME A PSYCHOTHERAPIST

BECOME A STEALTH PLANE TEST PILOT

Stealth planes are, as we
all know, invisible.

BE A TRIPOD

Camera tripods can look technical and threatening, unlike a friendly, smartly dressed corpse, which will put everyone at ease.

GO TRICK OR TREATING

Try a cute face to get the maximum amount of sweets.

HELP A TATTOOIST PRACTISE

Save others from a tattooist's
first clumsy attempts.

BECOME A WATER FEATURE

Bring a touch of ancient Rome to any garden or, if you must,
a touch of Brussels.

BECOME A VASE

You'll preserve the flowers even longer
with your own brand of compost.

WALK THE DOG

Don't just give the dog a bone – give him somebody to play with.

You'll cover up for your cheapskate friends who play their wedding disco off an iPod.